THE
MILLENNIUM

BUILDINGS

A Pictorial History of the
Past One Thousand Years

Sue Hamilton

ABDO
Daughters
&

Visit us at
www.abdopub.com

Published by ABDO Publishing Company, 4940 Viking Drive, Edina, MN 55435.
Copyright ©2000 by Abdo Consulting Group, Inc. International copyrights reserved in all countries. No part of this book may be reproduced in any form without written permission from the publisher.

Printed in the United States.

Art Direction: John Hamilton

Cover photos: AP/Wideworld Photos, Corbis
Interior photos: AP/Wideworld Photos, Corbis

Library of Congress Cataloging–in–Publication Data

Hamilton, Sue L., 1959-
      Buildings / Sue Hamilton.
             p. cm. -- (The millennium)
      Includes index.
      Summary: A pictorial history of developments in buildings over the last millennium.
      ISBN 1-57765-363-7
      1. Buildings--History--Juvenile literature. 2. Buildings--History--Pictorial works--Juvenile literature. [1. Buildings--History.] I. Title. II. Millennium (Minneapolis, Minn.)

NA2555 .H36 2000
720'.9--dc21

                                                                          99-057999

CONTENTS

INTRODUCTION

Throughout history, people have needed shelter from the elements. Early humans built primitive structures from mud, sticks, and stone. As the centuries progressed, builders used different materials to construct bigger and better buildings. Soon, the techniques of building simple structures evolved into the art of architecture as the needs of the people changed. Eventually, buildings provided not only shelter, but also provided the means of expressing and communicating ideas. At the end of the millennium, the art of building continued to evolve to suit the needs and communicate the messages of a changing society.

In the sixth century A.D., the Mayas built great stone cities like Chichén Itzá in Mexico. Above is Chichén Itzá's Temple of the Warriors.

Ancient Buildings

Early people built primitive buildings using materials that were available, usually mud, rocks, and sticks. Eventually, they learned to make bricks from mud and straw, and to fire them to make them stronger. The ancient Egyptians cut blocks from stone. They used these cut blocks to build the great pyramids.

Greek and Roman Buildings

The Greeks and Romans constructed buildings from stone. They were architectural pioneers, creating beautiful buildings with tall columns and intricate sculpture and carvings. The buildings of the Greeks and Romans created an architectural design style called Classical.

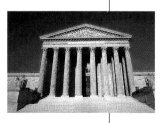

Asian Buildings

Early buildings in Asia were quite advanced. Temples and towers were built with wood, stone, and fired brick. These buildings had many stories and were very tall.

The Middle Ages

In Europe, the Middle Ages were a time of architectural triumph. Churches and castles took centuries to complete. Builders used stone arches to create buildings that were many stories tall. When builders figured out a new method of distributing roof weight, heavy walls were replaced with huge windows. Elaborate carvings and decoration added to the beauty of these mammoth structures.

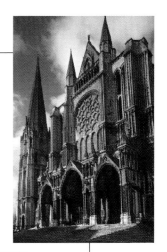

The Renaissance

The Renaissance was a time of creativity and discovery throughout Europe. Architects revived Greek and Roman architecture in their building designs. They also created new designs for homes. Builders continued to construct enormous cathedrals with detailed paintings and frescoes.

The Industrial Age

Buildings of the Industrial Age were designed to be efficient and modern. New construction materials, such as steel and iron frames, allowed buildings to grow taller and stronger. In the Industrial Age, people began to have more money and could afford to build bigger homes

The Eiffel Tower is an Industrial Age building constructed of wrought iron.

Modern Buildings

Lofty skyscrapers made of iron, steel, concrete, and glass began to appear in modern cities throughout the world. Architects moved away from classic Greek and Roman designs, creating buildings with unusual shapes and materials. At the end of the millennium, architects continued to design buildings to accommodate a modern lifestyle.

At over 1,300 feet tall (396 m), the World Trade Center's twin towers in New York City (left) are some of the highest in the world.

BEFORE THE MILLENNIUM

Early humans sought shelter in caves as well as in huts made of animal hides, sticks, and rocks. As the climate gradually warmed, people started farming. This led to the establishment of the first cities, which had buildings made of sun-dried mud bricks. As time went on, people experimented with new construction methods and materials. Their buildings grew larger and sturdier, and they developed sophisticated styles of architecture.

The Stone Age

The earliest humans sought shelter in caves. Scholars believe they lived near the mouth of the cave, while they may have used the deeper chambers for religious purposes such as painting sacred animals (right).

Terra Amata, located near Nice in southern France, shows proof of the first known human

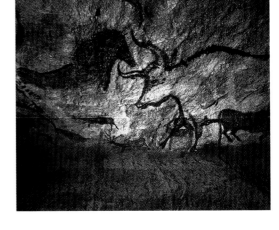

buildings. These structures are from 300,000 to 400,000 years ago. The oval-shaped huts are made of branches set close together in the sand (left). Outside, large stones were placed to brace the wooden sticks. Animal skins were used as door coverings.

The First Buildings

Around 10,000 B.C. in the Middle East, round buildings called *tholoi* (left) were made of packed clay. These Middle Eastern buildings probably had domed roofs that resembled a beehive.

In about 8000 B.C., the city of Jericho was built with mud bricks (right), which were molded by hand and dried in the sun. Firing bricks would come much later.

In ancient Greece, a tholos was a round building most likely used as a tomb. These buildings represented the beginning of masonry construction.

In the Neolithic era, about 5,000 B.C., people built timber and mud houses. Timber posts were set in holes in the ground, and braced with roof beams. Boughs were woven in and out of the posts to complete the walls of the shelters. Gaps were filled with mud. The roof was covered with thatch or turf.

The tholos at the Treasury of Atreus in Mycenae

Early Cities

The first cities appeared near great rivers such as the Nile and the Tigris. Using materials at hand, people created prefabricated mud bricks to form rectangular buildings. Buildings became sturdier when people discovered that bricks made of mud and straw held together better.

Then in 3000 B.C., they discovered that firing bricks made them last even longer. Around 2575 B.C., cut-stone construction became popular.

Between 3000 and 2000 B.C., Mesopotamians began creating bigger buildings called ziggurats. Ziggurats are pyramid-shaped brick buildings. They have a staircase that leads to a temple on top of the structure. Two of the most famous ziggurats are the Tower of Babel (above) and the Ziggurat of Nanna (the Sumerian god of the moon) in the city of Ur (left).

The Egyptians

The Great Pyramids at Giza, Egypt, were built between 2550 and 2470 B.C. They were built of large limestone blocks. The limestone was mined in a quarry, dragged on wooden sledges to the Nile River, loaded on a boat, and transported down the river. When it arrived at the construction site, workers used earthen ramps to position the stones into place.

The Pharos of Alexandria (left) was completed in 279 B.C., after 20 years of work. This three-story lighthouse was built of white marble and is considered the world's first high-rise building. Reaching 350 feet (107 m) in height, its light could be seen from 35 miles (56 km) away. The building survived until the seventh century when it was destroyed by Arabs.

8

The Minoans

Between 1900 and 1400 B.C., the Minoans occupied the Greek island of Crete. They created a vast temple that featured many levels, corridors, and rooms. Tapering columns made of tree trunks held up the floor. They used horn-shaped decorations on the roof and painted their walls with frescoes of bulls.

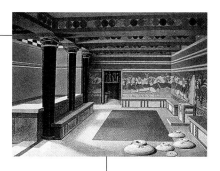

The Persians

In 575 B.C., King Nebuchadrezzar II's city of Babylon featured many wonders, including the Ishtar Gate (left), a true arch spanning 25 feet (8 m). The gate was made of colored glazed bricks and patterned with yellow and white bulls and dragons, which stood out from their blue background.

The Greeks

In the third century B.C., the Greeks invented the modern truss. A truss is a triangle-shaped frame used to support roofs. It can bear heavy loads and span great distances. The truss allowed builders to construct rooms that were larger than ever before.

The Greeks also developed three different kinds of columns: Doric, Ionic, and Corinthian. The columns surrounded the many Greek temples and continued to influence architecture at the end of the millennium.

The Parthenon (above, right), a temple to the Greek goddess Athena, was completed in 432 B.C. This temple is a rectangular building made of white marble and is surrounded by rows of columns on the outside. It is an example of Doric architecture.

The Etruscans

The Etruscans of northern Italy developed the first true stone arch.

The Porta Marzia, an arched city gateway in Perugia, Italy, built in the third century B.C.

The Romans

Romans mixed pozzolana with lime to form a strong cement that could harden even under water. The Temple of Sybil at Tivoli (left) was built using this concrete construction in the first century B.C.

Romans learned of the truss, a framework designed to support a roof, from the Greeks. Suddenly, rooms that were rarely larger than 25 feet (7.6 m) across, could span 75 feet (22.9 m).

Roman Emperor Nero built Domus Aurea *("Golden House"). One part of the palace was an octagonal hall topped by a concrete dome (right). It is believed to be the first such building created.*

The Colosseum in Rome, Italy, was built by the Roman Emperor Vespasian in A.D. 72 to present the skills of soldiers. The building was named after the Latin word colosseus. *The building was 620 feet (189 m) across and could hold over 50,000 spectators. It was made of concrete, brick, and stone, and the floor was made of wood covered with sand. A huge canvas canopy shaded the spectators, although little is known about how it was held in place.*

The Pantheon (right) was completed in A.D. 124 and featured a concrete dome that was 142 feet (43 m) across and 71 feet (22 m) high. It held the record for being the largest dome until the nineteenth century.

The Basilica of Constantine at Trier, completed in A.D. 313, featured the timber truss. This building also featured hypocaust, *a central heating system using hot air ducts in the floors.*

The Inuit

The Inuit igloo was often made of hide or sod over a wood or whalebone frame when the igloo was a permanent residence. The Inuit used snow and ice to construct temporary shelters.

The Native Americans

The Navajo made log houses covered with earth called hogans (right). The earth insulated the dwelling, keeping out the heat of summer. The traditional Navajo hogan is built around four posts, each representing one of the sacred mountains of their homeland. The doors on hogans face east to welcome the morning sun and to receive good blessings.

Native Americans of the Great Plains made tepees out of wooden poles and buffalo skins (left). Tepees had a hole in the top that allowed for ventilation. An inside liner kept the cold out. In the summer, the bottom of the tepee could be raised to allow the breeze to cool the interior. Tepees were easy to take down and put up, so when the people moved to follow game they could take their tepees with them.

The Chinese

From A.D. 581 to 907, the Chinese developed advanced building techniques. Temples featured heavy timber framing and high-rise pagoda towers were made of stone and fired brick.

The Big Wild Goose Pagoda in China was built in 652. The square pyramid is made of blue brick, has seven stories, and is 210 feet high (64 m).

Built in A.D. 586, the Longxing Temple is the biggest Buddhist temple in north China. It covers an area of 689,000 square feet (64,000 sq m).

1000 TO 1100

Beginning in the eleventh century, Europeans built many massive churches and castles in the Romanesque style of architecture. These buildings usually were made of stone and had domes, arches, and vaulting. During this time period in the Middle East, people built lofty towers. In Asia, buildings with detailed carvings appeared.

Europe

Churches and state military buildings featured the Romanesque style of building with stone arches and domes. An example of the Romanesque style is the Speyer Cathedral (left) in Germany's Rhineland. It was built in the eleventh century. The abbey church of St. Philibert, in Tournus, France (below), also featured Romanesque styles, such as a nave with vaulted ceilings and huge pillars built after a fire in 1066.

The interior of St. Philibert, showing a nave of vaulted ceilings and pillars

The Middle East

Tomb towers were popular in Iran during the eleventh and twelfth centuries. One example is the Gonbad-e Qabus (left), a 200-foot (61-m) high star-shaped design built of brick in A.D. 1006 to 1007.

Tall cylindrical towers were built in Iran (right). At first these detailed brick towers were used to celebrate special events or victorious battles.

Later they were used as landmarks to mark important travel routes across the country.

Armenian architecture features the use of colored stones cut into small squares. The Cathedral of Ani (below), completed in 1001, features warm shades of stone on four sides.

Asia

An example of Hindu architecture, the Kandarya Mahadeva Temple in Khajuraho, central India, was completed in about 1050. It had over 80 buildings. It featured a main tower that is 116 feet (35 m) high. The sandstone buildings feature elaborate carvings in bands called friezes.

In East Asia, dome-shaped Buddhist burial monuments called temples were built. The tower of the Ananda temple (right) in Pagan, Burma, started in A.D. 1091, has a central tower.

1100 TO 1200

The Kutubiya Mosque in Marrakesh, Morocco, features the complex styles of Islamic architecture.

During the twelfth century, buildings continued to grow in sophistication and in size. In Asia, builders created a massive religious monument. Castle construction evolve in Europe and the Middle East, creating castles that were easier to defend. Builders continued to construct enormous churches in Europe.

A moat and three galleries encircle the five central shrines.

Asia

Angkor Wat (left) is the majestic work of Suryavarman II (1113-c. 1150). It is one of the largest religious monuments ever built. The temple complex covers an astounding 77 square miles (200 sq km). The central monument represents the sacred Mount Meru, and the five towers symbolize Mount Meru's five peaks.

The Middle East

The knights of St. John built *Krak Des Chevaliers* (Castle of the Knights—right) in Syria. The castle has two circular sets of walls separated by a wide moat, providing maximum security. The castle could house two thousand soldiers.

Europe

Construction of the Pisa Cathedral (right) in Pisa, Italy, began in 1173. The cathedral's bell tower was designed to be vertical, but started to incline during its construction. The weight of the building on a small base caused the foundation to sink into the ground. It leans 17 feet (5.2 m) from top to base. At the end of the millennium, efforts were still being made to halt the leaning of the tower.

In England, the Durham Cathedral (left) was completed in 1133. It is the first major English structure to be vaulted entirely in stone (right).

Stave churches were built in Europe where there was still a lot of timber. One of the oldest surviving stave churches is found in Borgund, Norway (below, left), which was completed in 1150. The stone foundation supports four horizontal wooden beams from which rise four corner posts, or staves. These designs were masterpieces of woodworking, with wooden braces, trusses, and cross beams all arranged to support the building.

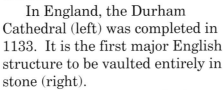

In northern Europe, many motte and bailey castles (right) were built. The motte was a hill. At the top was a guard tower made of timber. Surrounding it was the bailey, an enclosure that protected the tower and other buildings. At the bottom of the hill was a palisade, a fence made of stakes or pointed sticks. These castles were easy to defend and hard to attack.

1200 TO 1300

During the thirteenth century, Europeans built massive cathedrals in the Gothic style of architecture. These cathedrals featured flying buttresses, stained-glass windows, and pointed arches. In the Middle East, castle construction continued to improve, and in South America the Incas built a mountain-top city using giant pieces of stone. In Asia, people constructed homes that could be built and taken down quickly. Africa saw the construction of stone churches.

Paris's Notre-Dame (above) is a Gothic cathedral built from 1163-1250.

Europe

In Northern France a new type of cathedral was created in the early 1200s. These Gothic-style cathedrals were very detailed, with turrets, canopies, and relief sculpture (upper right).

One of the major innovations of the Gothic style was the flying buttress (right). The flying

buttress is a system of piers and arches that relieve pressure from the roof, allowing the cathedrals to have thinner walls. With thinner walls, cathedrals could be filled with large, stained-glass windows (left).

The Middle East

Northern Syria's Citadel of Aleppo (right) had a massive rectangular gate-tower, which was reached by a narrow, tall bridge. The existing citadel was erected in 1209 atop fortifications from Byzantine, Roman, and earlier times. It was designed for defense during the time of the Crusades.

South America

Machu Picchu (right), in the Andes Mountains of Peru, dates to A.D. 1200. Enormous pieces of stone were transported over the mountains, then precisely cut to fit together without mortar. This was an example of Cyclopean masonry.

Asia

The nomads of Mongolia lived in yurts in the thirteenth century, as many still did at the end of the millennium. These tent-like dwellings are made of lattice-framed wooden poles covered with skins or thick felt and anchored with ropes. Inside, brightly colored woven rugs cover the floor. Yurts can be built and taken down quickly.

A yurt

Africa

Emperor Lalibela of Ethiopia built 11 rock-cut subterranean churches. The churches were hewn from solid rock from the top down. The Beit Giorgis (Church of St. George) is cross-shaped (left). It remains an important place for Christians to visit.

The Elliptical Building in Great Zimbabwe, East Africa, was enclosed in high dry-stone walls (right). These walls were fitted together without mortar. Soapstone pillars with carved birds (left) were placed along the top of the walls.

The Conical Tower at Great Zimbabwe

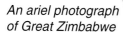

An ariel photograph of Great Zimbabwe

1300 TO 1400

During the fourteenth century, building construction continued to advance. Native Americans constructed longhouses and pueblos. In Europe, people began using a new form of home construction, and the jobs of designer and builder became separate. In Central America, indigenous people produced decorative stonework.

North America

The Iroquoi of northeastern North America built communal longhouses. Howlett Hill in New York shows the remains of a longhouse that was more than 328 feet (100 m) long. It was made from a pole frame that was covered with sheets of bark. Many families lived in a longhouse. Each family had its own section and hearth.

Pueblos, a term used by Spanish explorers, first appeared in the American Southwest around A.D. 1300. Pueblo walls were made of adobe, a mixture of clay and water, that was formed into bricks and dried in the sun. The thick walls provided excellent insulation, keeping the dwellings cool in the summer and warm in the winter. Pueblos sheltered hundreds of families.

The Taos Pueblo in Taos, New Mexico, is one of the oldest continuously inhabited communities in the United States.

Europe

Half-timber construction became a new form of house building in the fourteenth century. It featured wooden beams that held the building up. These beams remained visible and became part of the building's design. The space between the beams was filled with brick, plaster, or wattle and daub. This would become the standard for wooden home construction in Europe until the nineteenth century.

Europeans began to make fired bricks again in the fourteenth century, although the precise techniques of ancient brickmaking had been lost. The bricks of the fourteenth century often distorted and were expensive because of the fuel needed to fire them. The bricks were bonded together with mortar.

One of the first buildings in which the designer and the builder were separate persons was the Campanile of the Cathedral of Florence (left). The famous Italian painter Giotto designed the building, while cathedral masons constructed it from 1334 to 1359.

The Palace of Westminster was built at the end of the fourteenth century. It was originally to be used as a royal residence. It eventually became the headquarters for the British government. Westminster Hall (right) featured a 70-foot (21.3-m) wide wooden hammerbeam roof, considered an amazing feat of carpentry for the time.

Central America

During the fourteenth century, the Mixtecs of Mexico's Oaxaca region took existing walls and applied beautiful ornamental stonework (left). The city of Mitla, Mexico, displayed many of their brightly painted geometric mosaics (right).

1400 TO 1500

Italian architect Leon Battista Alberti (above) wrote and published Ten Books on Architecture, *the first books on the subject since Vitruvius, a Roman from the first century* B.C.

The Renaissance began in Italy in the fourteenth century, influencing European architects for hundreds of years. Renaissance architects designed buildings that were inspired by the styles of classic Greek and Roman societies. In Asia, builders constructed an umbrella-shaped temple. In the Middle East, people built houses with private courtyards.

Asia

Chinese emperors built *Tian Tan* (the Temple of Heaven) around 1420. The Temple is about 1 mile (2 km) southeast of the Forbidden City in Beijing.

The Temple of Heaven has an area of 675 acres (273 ha). Two walls divide the ground into inner and outer parts. The umbrella-like structure of three tiers stands on a twenty-foot high (6 m) white marble circular terrace and is 105 feet (32 m) high and 79 feet (24 m) around at the base.

The Temple of Heaven

The Middle East

Reflecting the wealth of the land, huge courtyard houses were built in Cairo, Egypt. They were made of fine ashlar, with wrought-iron window grills and timber balconies. The central courtyard displayed the events of the household. Outside, however, the houses showed only a plain wall, designed for security and privacy.

Europe

Florence Cathedral in Italy (left) was considered the greatest engineering feat of its time. Its eight-sided dome was designed by Filippo Brunelleschi and built without the use of scaffolding. Dedicated to *Santa Maria Del Fiore* (Our Lady of the Flower), its style was Florentine, with patters of red, green, and white marble on its exterior walls.

Wealthy fifteenth-century families in Italy began living in a new building style called a *palazzo*. The Palazzo Rucellai (1451 to 1455), designed by Leon Battista Alberti, was built several stories high (right). The walls surrounded an inside courtyard. The outer wall featured pilasters, which provided the space for windows.

Construction on the King's College Chapel (left) in Cambridge, England, began in 1446 and continued until 1515. It is an example of one of the last English buildings in the Gothic style. The inside displays a web of beauty and delicacy called fan vaulting (right), built by master mason John Wastell.

Ivan the Great, first Tsar of Russia, hired the Italian architect Aristotle Fioravanti to build a series of cathedrals in Moscow. The Cathedral of the Annunciation (left) featured nine gilded domes, and reflected Italian and Russian styles of architecture.

1500 TO 1600

I n the sixteenth century, European architects continued to draw inspiration from classical societies. Architects and builders created the largest church in the world. And, the construction of a new theater set the standard for future theater designs.

Dwellings like the Villa Rotunda in 1571 (above), created by Palladio, emphasized the styles of Roman architecture in clean, clear lines.

Europe

Although people in other lands had constructed domed roofs in the past, the Romans took dome construction to a new level. They introduced masonry construction of the large-scale dome. St. Peter's Basilica (left) was built in the sixteenth and seventeenth centuries in Vatican City, Rome. The church features a giant ribbed dome designed by Michelangelo that is 435 feet (133 m) tall. At the time it was the largest church in the world.

Donato Bramante built the Tempietto San Pietro (right) for Pope Julius II from 1502-1510. This stone temple in Rome is a circular, domed shrine without outside decoration. Bramante combined the Roman ideals of simple dignity with Renaissance elegance.

Commissioned by Tsar Ivan IV, St. Basil's Cathedral (left) in Moscow was built from 1555 to 1560. It was really nine churches: one main one surrounded by eight smaller chapels, with brilliantly-colored onion domes and belfries.

Italian architect Giorgio Vasari borrowed from Roman technology and used king-post timber trusses

to create a 66-foot (20-m) roof span in the Uffizi Palace (left and right). It was built originally in the mid-sixteenth century as a government office building.

The Countess of Shrewsbury built Hardwick Hall (right) in Derbyshire, England, in 1597. It was a country house of brick, stone, and timber that was an example of Elizabethan architecture. Inside it featured a High Great Chamber with a plaster frieze of scenes from the Garden of Eden, an elaborate stairway, and large windows overlooking the gardens and surrounding lands.

The Teatro Olimpico (left) was an indoor theatre whose design became the model for all theaters and opera houses thereafter. When complete in 1594, the horseshoe-shaped auditorium featured tiered seating with rows of classical columns surrounding the area. Overhead, the ceiling was painted to look like the sky. Statues of members of the Olympian Academy overlooked the stage from above.

1600 TO 1700

English architect Sir Christopher Wren

I n the seventeenth century, much Asian architecture used plain, simple designs that utilized natural building materials. In Europe, a new style of architecture called the Baroque style evolved. Baroque style was very elaborate. Colored marble, detailed paintings, sculpture, and gilding ornamented buildings in this period.

Asia

When the Mughal Emperor Shah Jahan's wife died in childbirth in 1631, he spent 23 years building her a resting place like no other. The Taj Mahal is made of marble-clad brick and is exactly the same on both sides. The building's symmetry is broken only in the tomb area, where Jahan's resting place is slightly higher than his wife's.

The Taj Mahal (above) is decorated in flower patterns using semiprecious stones and calligraphy from the Koran.

The Katsura Detached Palace (left and right), in Koyoto, Japan, was built from 1620-58. The palace was designed to work with the natural surroundings of the building. It was made of wood with whitewashed walls and sliding screens that opened onto the gardens.

The texture of the materials used in its building are the Katsura Palace's only decoration.

Potala Palace sits high on a plateau in Lhasa, Tibet. The White Palace (1645-90) was built by the fifth Dalai Lama to be used for

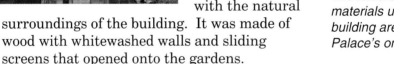

The gilding in the Shrine Hall contains 4.25 tons (3.86 t) of gold.

state functions and as apartments. It encircles the Red Palace (1690-94), which holds sacred relics, and holy tombs. The rough stone walls rise 13 stories up the side of the mountain. The gilded turrets are decorated with symbols showing victory over the world's suffering.

Europe

After London's Great Fire in 1666, Sir Christopher Wren was commissioned to build a new St. Paul's Cathedral on the site of the old one. He created a Baroque-style church dominated by an elevated, central rotunda and a beautiful outer dome. With fluid, balanced design, St. Paul's represented the most advanced works of structural design created to date.

The Banqueting House (1619-22) in Whitehall, England (right), was architect Inigo Jones's masterpiece. It contains the first recorded use of crown glass windows. Glassblowers spun molten glass into disks, let it cool, polished it, and then cut it into rectangles. This marked the beginning of the generous use of glass in buildings.

King Louis XIV of France displayed his power and wealth through the building of Versailles Palace, beginning in 1660. It has 2,143 windows, 1,252 fireplaces, and 67 staircases. The gardens included roughly 1,400 fountains.

One of the best-known features is the Hall of Mirrors (right). The mirrors on one wall matched up with the garden-facing windows on the opposite wall. Natural light could be seen everywhere.

North America

Boston was already a growing city when the original Boston Town House was built from 1657 to 1658. Similar to medieval town halls, it featured an open-walled public market on the ground floor and meeting rooms above.

1700 TO 1800

The eighteenth century was a time of transition. Increased education, scientific discoveries, and a focus on the arts made this period known as the Age of Enlightenment. While the Baroque style was still in use, architects began to explore other designs. New knowledge in the West of ancient Greek and Roman buildings sparked a new style of design called Neoclassical. The mid-century arrival of the Industrial Age created a need for a type of industrial design.

North America

Before becoming the third president of the United States, Thomas Jefferson designed and built Monticello. This mountain-top home was built in Charlottesville, Virginia, from 1769 to 1784. Jefferson used Roman and Palladian designs, significantly influencing the architecture of America.

Asia

The Jantar Mantar observatory in Jaipur, India, was completed in 1734. It consists of fourteen major geometric devices for measuring time, predicting eclipses, tracking stars in their orbits, ascertaining the declinations of planets, and determining the celestial altitudes. The instruments are built of local stone and marble, and each instrument carries an astronomical scale, generally marked on the marble inner lining.

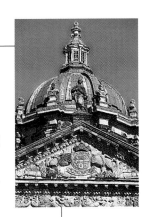

Europe

Castle Howard (left and right) was built throughout the 1700s in Yorkshire, England. It was designed by Sir John Vanbrugh and Nicholas Hawksmoor. The castle's bold decoration of large statues and elaborate carvings are an example of English Baroque architecture.

Claude-Nicolas Ledoux created the first example of industrial architecture in France when he built the royal salt factory, Arc-et-Senans (right). The industrial city was built in concentric circles containing shops and housing, with the director's house right in the middle. The salt factory contained everything a worker needed and facilitated production efficiency.

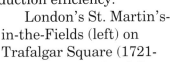

London's St. Martin's-in-the-Fields (left) on Trafalgar Square (1721-26) is an example of Georgian-style architecture. James Gibbs designed the church, and its steeple was duplicated throughout North America.

Large-scale iron provided builders with a new construction material. In 1772, St. Anne's Church (right) in Liverpool, England, was one of the first structures to use solid cast-iron columns in its building construction.

Robert Adam designed simple, light spacious buildings in a Neoclassic style. He remodeled Syon House and Osterley Park House in the 1760s. In Syon House (left), he created a Roman anteroom filled with twelve green marble columns decorated with gilding.

1800 TO 1850

The Industrial Age created many successful businesses. All over the world, many people were able to afford big beautiful homes. In Europe, gas lighting was developed, and the widespread availability of iron prompted its use in building design. While some architects focused on industrial design, many looked to the past for ideas. This prompted the Greek classical style, with Doric and Ionic columns and simple ornamentation. And in England, the Gothic design style made a comeback.

North America

In the 1820s, sawmills began to use steam and water-powered saws to cut uniform-sized pieces of lumber. In the 1830s, machine-made nails were invented. The combination of these two developments, plus the large supply of lumber in North America, led to balloon-frame construction.

The first balloon-framed building is thought to have been a Chicago warehouse built in 1832. In this type of construction, studs extended the length of the structure, from the foundation to the rafters. Floor boards were then nailed to the studs. This vertical-style of construction was inexpensive, fast, and easy to build even with unskilled crews. It became popular across the Midwest and was used for houses and barns.

Balloon-frame construction is most common in North America, where wood supplies are plentiful.

Europe

In 1815, England's Prince of Wales asked architect John Nash to add to his country house in the oriental style of Mogul India. The Brighton Royal

Pavilion seaside resort (above, left) featured onion-shaped domes, tent-like roofs, and minarets. Nash used a cast-iron framework to provide the form of the dome, the "bamboo" staircase (right), and the "palm-tree" columns. This was the first recorded use of cast iron in a home's interior.

William Murdock developed a gas jet lighting fixture in 1792. In 1803, inventor James Watt's foundry in Birmingham, England, was the first large building with gas lighting. The power source was a small gas plant on the site.

Berlin, Germany's Altes Museum (right) reintroduced classical Greek styles. Architect Karl Schinkel designed this art museum, which

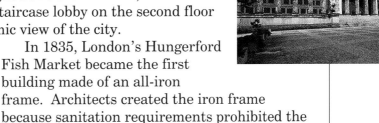

features an open staircase lobby on the second floor framing a panoramic view of the city.

In 1835, London's Hungerford Fish Market became the first building made of an all-iron frame. Architects created the iron frame because sanitation requirements prohibited the use of timber.

Architect Decimus Burton designed the next building to have an iron frame, the Palm House (right) at Kew Gardens near London. This 1840s greenhouse, built of glass and iron, allowed for a sunny, warm environment for tropical plants, even during England's cold weather.

A huge fire in 1834 destroyed most of the Palace of Westminster in London. In its place, architect Sir Charles Barry designed the Houses of Parliament at Westminster (left). He built them in the Gothic Revival style.

1850 TO 1900

Builders were using iron frames to bring structures to heights that they had not been able to achieve in the past. Iron arches made the interior of buildings bigger than ever before. The invention of the elevator in America paved the way for even taller buildings. While the industrialization of the world continued, some builders still modeled their buildings on those from the past.

North America

Elisha Otis's 1852 invention of the safety elevator allowed architects to design taller buildings. This, together with the high cost of land in a city, brought a new demand on architects: to develop buildings with great height.

In 1884, William Le Baron Jenney designed Chicago's 10-story Home Insurance Company Building (above, left). It had a metal skeleton of cast-iron columns, wrought-iron beams, and masonry walls. Chicago featured many skyscrapers in the late 1890s, including the Reliance Building (14 stories) and the Carson Pirie Scott Store (12 stories).

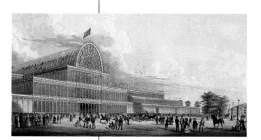

Europe

Sir Joseph Paxton designed the Crystal Palace for the Great Exhibition in Hyde Park, London. It was made of cast and wrought iron, timber, and glass that allowed the maximum of natural light. The design used prefabricated materials, which allowed for the giant exhibit hall to be built in only six months.

Charles Garnier created the Paris Opera House, which opened on January 5, 1875. From the grand staircase (above right) made of marble, onyx, and bronze, to the huge central dome, it was indeed a work of art.

Alexandre-Gustave Eiffel built an amazing tower in 1889 that served as the entranceway to an exhibit celebrating 100 years since the French Revolution. The Eiffel Tower (shown at left in various phases of construction) was made of thousands of prefabricated, wrought iron cross braces that held the structure rigid. Even though the tower is 984 feet tall (300 m), the design keeps it from swaying in the wind.

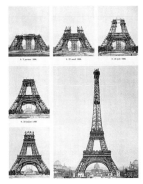

The Eiffel Tower has 15,000 parts held together with over 2.5 million rivets, and weighs 9,441 tons (9592.5 metric tons).

The Galerie des Machines (Gallery of Machines) was a glass building also built for the Paris Exhibition of 1889. It featured a series of three-hinged trussed arches. The glass-enclosed clear span of 536,000 square feet (49,790 sq m) has never been equaled.

King Ludwig II began building Neuschwanstein Castle in 1869. The castle was a reconstruction of a medieval castle. It had towers, turrets, and battlements. But it was much more "modern" than the castles of old, with a central heating system and hot and cold running water.

Walt Disney modeled Sleeping Beauty's castle after Neuschwanstein.

The Galerie des Machines was so big, it was not suitable for other tenants after the Exhibition. It was demolished in 1910.

1900 TO 1920

The turn of the century brought many new architectural innovations. Art Nouveau style incorporated iron and glass, with wavy, asymmetrical lines that were often in the form of flower vines, leaves, and petals. The Arts and Crafts movement attempted to offset the effects of the industrialization of architectural design, and the Prairie Style design of low, horizontal lines, ribbon windows, and wide, overhanging eaves debuted in America.

Europe

Jahrhunderthalle (left) was built in 1913 in Wroclow, Poland, to commemorate the 100th anniversary of the uprising against Napoleon. The enormous building has a clear span of 216 feet (66 m). Jahrhunderthalle's architect, Max Berg, was one of the first to use concrete to create this type of long-span building.

Spanish architect Antoni Gaudi designed several buildings in the Art Nouveau style. His works, such as the 1907 apartment buildings of Casa Batlló (above, left) and the Casa Milá (right), featured curved, wavelike roofs and spires adorned with mosaics.

In 1916, during World War I, French engineer Eugène Freyssinet created airship hangers in Orly, near Paris. Reinforced concrete was shaped into arches and pierced with windows. The huge hangers could hold airplanes and dirigibles.

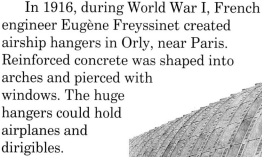

North America

The Flatiron Building (right), designed by Daniel Burnham, is a 21-story triangular skyscraper in New York City. It was completed in 1901 and is considered New York City's first skyscraper.

Brothers Henry and Charles Greene created a new style of home when they designed the California bungalow, a one-story house with a low-pitched roof. This design and variations of it influenced the design of countless homes.

The Greene brothers are also well-known for the Gamble House (left) in Pasadena, California. The brothers not only designed the house but also designed all of its furnishings. It was completed in 1908 and represents the American Arts and Crafts style of architecture.

Frank Lloyd Wright designed the Frederick C. Robie House (right) in 1909. In the Robie House, Wright eliminated the box-type room design by using windows on exterior walls and an open floor plan to create a light, flowing, transparent living space. Wright also incorporated all the newest innovations, including connective heating, electric lighting, and early air-conditioning.

Named after the inventor of the cable car, Andrew S. Hallidie, the Hallidie Building (1918, left) of San Francisco was the first to use an all-glass curtain wall. It was the forerunner of structures made with glass.

1920 TO 1940

The early part of the twentieth century brought new architectural styles that turned away form traditional designs. Modern architecture rejected the ornamentation and decoration that was characteristic of past building styles while utilizing the building material of the Industrial Age, such as glass, iron, steel, and concrete. From this movement, Art Deco evolved, utilizing simple, clean shapes to suggest the elegance and sophistication that heavy ornamentation did in the past.

Europe

The Schröder House (1925) in Utrecht, the Netherlands, represents early modern architecture. Gerrit Rietveld designed the steel-frame brick and concrete house, which makes use of three-dimensional grids of space and color. It includes a roof glass lantern that lights the center of the house.

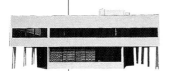

In 1930, Charles-Édouard Le Corbusier designed the Savoye House in Poissy, France, which displays the Modern Movement design in architecture. The house's square, white concrete "ocean-liner" exterior and windowed walls emphasize volume and natural light.

North America

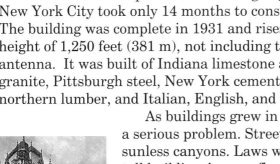

The 102-floor Empire State Building (right) in New York City took only 14 months to construct. The building was complete in 1931 and rises to a height of 1,250 feet (381 m), not including the antenna. It was built of Indiana limestone and granite, Pittsburgh steel, New York cement, northern lumber, and Italian, English, and German marble.

As buildings grew in height, New York faced a serious problem. Streets had turned into sunless canyons. Laws were put into place, and tall buildings' upper floors were required to be pulled back in a series of setbacks.

The Chrysler Building in 1930 (right) and the Waldorf Astoria Hotel in 1931 (left) featured fancy crowning features based on city requirements and beautiful designs.

Frank Lloyd Wright continued his innovative designs. Fallingwater (1938, left), halfway between the villages of Mill Run and Ohiopyle, Pennsylvania, was built over a waterfall. It incorporated his "natural" design with rough stone walls. The Johnson Wax Building (right) in Racine, Wisconsin, incorporated the use of translucent tubes of Pyrex glass to illuminate the inside of the Great Workroom with natural light.

Interior of the Johnson Wax Building

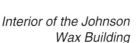

1940 TO 1960

During the mid-twentieth century, much of Europe worked to rebuild after the devastation of World War II. This new construction enabled architects to explore new design options. Buildings had unusual shapes, and were built with exciting new materials like aluminum and smoked glass.

Europe

Le Corbusier was asked to rebuild a pilgrimage chapel in the Vosges mountains in France. He produced Notre-Dame-du-Haut (right). The hull-like form is turned up to resemble a three-cornered hat. It floats over curving, tapered walls.

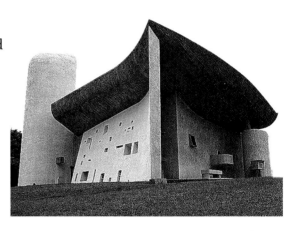

South America

In 1958, Oscar Niemeyer developed a dynamic style of design in the presidential Palace of the Alvorada in Brasília, Brazil.

North America

Le Corbusier designed New York's United Nations Secretariat Building (1949, left). The building had green-tinted glass walls and a Weather-master air-conditioning system. It set the standard for tall buildings around the world.

Ludwig Mies van der Rohe designed the Seagram Building (right) in New York City using curtain-wall construction of black anodized aluminum and smoked glass. It was completed in 1958.

Architect Philip Johnson built his own "house of glass" (left) in 1949. The Connecticut home was the first of its kind, built entirely of transparent glass, except for one central bathroom that was enclosed in a cylinder.

Mies combined a structural-steel frame and a glass box, creating the Farnsworth House (1950, right) on the Fox River in Plano, Illinois. It featured full-length plate glass windows. The walls appeared transparent until silk curtains were added for privacy.

Frank Lloyd Wright produced the Guggenheim Museum (left) in New York City. It was a circular-shaped art museum made of concrete. Its ramps wind upward, displaying paintings on the walls (right). At the top is a glass dome that lets in natural light (bottom, left).

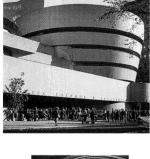

1960 TO 1980

Near the end of the twentieth century, architects all over the world were using building materials in new ways. New types of arches, innovative use of concrete, and the utilization of unusual materials such as fabric created buildings that were different from anything in the past.

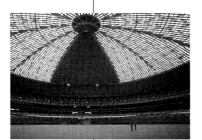

North America

In 1964, Houston, Texas, became the home of one of the first great covered sports stadiums: the Astrodome (left). The 642-foot (195.7-m) lamella dome was made of intersecting arches hinged together at their midpoints to form an interlocking diamond pattern.

Built in the late 1960s, Chicago's 100-story John Hancock Building (right) is 1,127 feet (343.5 m) high. Engineer Fazlur Khan's used an innovative system of outside diagonal bracing. This bundled tube construction was so efficient, the building required significantly less steel to be built.

In 1976, the world's tallest freestanding structure was completed. The Canadian National Railway's CN Tower in Toronto was designed to allow radio and TV signals to be transmitted without interference from other buildings.

The CN Tower (left) was created using a huge mold known as a slip form. Concrete was poured day and night, five days a week. As the concrete hardened, the mold moved upwards. The form gradually decreased, giving the tower its tapering shape.

Sitting at the top of the CN Tower is the Sky Pod, the highest public observation gallery in the world at 1,465 feet (447 m). With its antenna, the overall height of the CN Tower is 1,815 feet, 5 inches (553.33 m).

The John Hancock Building needed 29 pounds (13.2 kg) of steel per square foot, while the shorter 60-story Chase Manhattan Bank Building (top of page, left) required 55 pounds (24.9 kg) of steel per square foot.

Australia

In 1973, the Sydney Opera House in Australia was built by Jorn Utzon. Among its amazing features, it has overlapping roofs that remind people of sails on a boat.

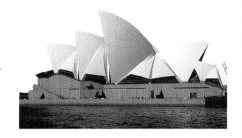

Europe

In Paris, the high-tech Georges Pompidou National Center for Art and Culture (left) was completed in 1977. It is a free-spanning structure, designed to allow for openness and flexibility. Vertical tubes carrying electricity, water, drainage, and air-handling ducts are all color-coded on the outside of the building.

Frei Otto designed arenas for the Olympic Village (right) in Munich, Germany, for the 1972 Olympic Games. The arenas were covered by vast awnings stretched with steel cables and covered with a transparent polyester fabric.

Asia

Kenzo Tenge designed the sports stadium for the 1964 Olympic Games in Tokyo, Japan. The Tokyo Olympic Stadium became a combination of modern and traditional Japanese architecture. The reinforced concrete building featured a suspended roof structure with skylights.

1980 TO 2000

At the close of the twentieth century, architects continued to experiment with design and materials to improve buildings' looks and function. At the turn of the twenty-first century, architects faced problems such as overpopulation, excessive noise, and parking shortages. But architects and builders continued to employ the innovation and creativity that brought buildings from grass and stone huts to towering skyscrapers to solve the problems of a global society in a new millennium.

Asia

Sir Norman Foster's Hong Kong and Shanghai Bank (1981-85) was made of glass panels consisting of sandwiched layers of glass and fine mesh. The panels incorporate canopies that control direct glare and prevent overheating inside the building.

The 12-story internal atrium is lit by the glass end wall, which allows natural light to be reflected into the building. The outside features coat-hanger trusses every eight-stories, which provide stability to the building.

The world's largest planetarium is in the Ehime Prefectural Science Museum (left) in Niihama City, Japan. The museum's futuristic buildings were designed by Kisho Kurokawa. The planetarium is 98 feet (30 m) in diameter. Also included in the complex are cone-shaped entrance halls, a cubic exhibition hall, two crescent-shaped buildings for restaurants, and study rooms.

At the end of the millennium, the 1,483 foot (452 m) Petronas Towers (right) in Kuala Lumpur, Malaysia, were acknowledged by the Council on Tall Buildings and Urban Habitat as the tallest buildings in the world.

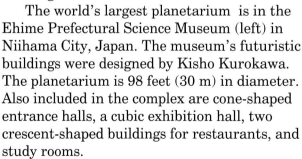

North America

The people of Cleveland, Ohio, wanted a building that would make as much of a statement as the artists honored inside the Rock and Roll Hall of Fame. They achieved that with Ieoh Ming Pei's eclectic modern museum (right), which opened in 1995. The pyramid-shaped, glass-clad building is a typical Pei design.

In 1982, Minneapolis, Minnesota, became the home of the first major league air-supported dome: the Hubert H. Humphrey Metrodome (left). The dome is covered by more than 10 acres (4 ha) of Teflon-coated fiberglass fabric. Fans enter through revolving doors that prevent the release of the air that keeps the dome upright.

Europe

Completed in 1992, the Ark (right) is a London office building that's design provides bright, open workspaces, while cutting off the noise and pollution of the surrounding area. Ralph Erskine designed the curved "skin" of the walls to reflect noise.

Sir James Stirling designed the Neue Staatsgalerie (left), an art gallery with both Classical and Modernist architectural styles. The building sits on a podium which conceals the ground floor parking area. Made of masonry, steel, and reinforced concrete, the building forms a U-shape, enclosing a sculpture terrace. The building was completed in 1984.

Valencia, Spain, is the home of a new educational entertainment center called La Ciudad de las Artes y las Ciencias (left). Santiago Calatrava created this park built in the shape of a gigantic open eye. The buildings are made of metal and glass and look so delicate they seem to appear weightless. The Universal Oceanographic Park recreates marine habitats. The areas are connected by submarine glass walkways.

BUILDINGS

Cathedral of Ani completed in Armenia (1001); Gonbad-e Qabus completed in Iran (1007)

Kandarya Mahadeva Temple completed (1050); Ananda temple tower completed (1091)

Speyer Cathedral built in Germany; Castle of Knights in Syria built; Stave churches and motte and bailey castles built in Europe; Durham Cathedral completed (1133)

Angkor Wat completed (1150); Borgund, Norway, stave church (1150)

1000   1050   1100   1150   1200

Batista publishes book on architecture; Brunelleschi designs Florence Cathedral; Cathedral of the Annunciation built in Moscow; Tian Tan completed in China (1420)

Palazzo Rucellai completed in Italy (1455)

Construction begins on St. Peter's Basilica in Rome; Tempietto San Pietro completed in Rome (1510)

St. Basil's Cathedral in Moscow completed (1560); Uffizi Palace completed; Villa Rotunda built (1571); Teatro Olimpico completed (1584); Hardwick Hall completed (1597)

1400   1450   1500   1550   1600

Altes museum reintroduces Greek architecture; Watt's foundry first large building to use gas light (1803)

Brighton Royal Pavilion (1815)

The first powered sawmills

Machine-made nails; Britain's Houses of Parliament built; first balloon frame building built in Chicago (1832); Hungerford Fish Market (1835)

Palm House built at Kew Gardens

1800   1810   1820   1830   1840   1850

Flatiron Building in New York (1901); Casa Batlló and Casa Milá built (1907); Gamble House (1908); Frederick C. Robie House built (1909)

First long span building made of concrete: Jahrhunderthalle (1913); airship hangars (1916); first all glass curtain wall: Hallidie Building (1918)

Schröder House built (1925)

Savoye House, Chrysler Building (1930); Waldorf-Astoria Hotel, Empire State Building (1931); Fallingwater (1938); Johnson Wax Building (1939)

United Nations Secretariat Building, Johnson's "house of glass" (1949)

1900   1910   1920   1930   1940   1950

MILESTONES

Mongolian yurts; Gothic Cathedrals; Elliptical Building built in East Africa; Subterranean churches built in Ethiopia; Machu Picchu built (1200); Citadel of Aleppo built (1209)	Notre Dame of Paris completed (1250) 	Iroquois build longhouses; Half-timber construction in Europe; Europeans fire bricks; Mixtec carve stone; Pueblos built in American Southwest	Campanile of the Cathedral of Florence (1359); Palace of Westminster in England

1200   1250   1300   1350   1400

Taj Mahal built in India; Banqueting House completed in England (1622) 	Potala Palace in Tibet: White Palace completed in 1690, Red Palace completed in 1694; Boston Town House, Katura Detached Palace (1658); Construction begins on Versailles Palace (1660)	Castle Howard; Arc-et-Senans salt factory built; St. Martin's-in-the-Fields (1726); Jantar Mantar Observatory (1734)	Syon House remodeled; Monticello (1784); St. Anne's church (1772); Murdock develops gas lighting (1792)

1600   1650   1700   1750   1800

Crystal Palace (1851); Otis invents the safety elevator (1852) 	Neuschwanstein Castle (1869) 	Paris Opera House (1875) 	First skyscraper: Home Insurance Company building (1884); Eiffel Tower and Galerie des Machines built (1889)

1850   1860   1870   1880   1890   1900

Farnsworth House (1950); Seagram Building, Palace of the Alvorada (1958); Wright's Solomon R. Guggenheim Museum (1959)	Houston Astrodome, Sports Stadium for Tokyo Olympics (1964); John Hancock Building	Olympic Village, Munich (1972); Sidney Opera House (1973); CN Tower (1976); Georges Pompidou National Center for the Arts (1977)	HHH Metrodome (1982); Neue Staatsgalerie finished in Germany (1984); Hong Kong and Shanghai Bank building (1985)	Petronas Towers; Ark office building (1992); Rock-n-Roll Hall of Fame (1995) 

1950   1960   1970   1980   1990   2000

GLOSSARY

anodize - to coat a metal with a decorative or protective film through the use of an electric current.

antenna - a metal device used to receive or transmit radio or television signals.

anteroom - a waiting room or entrance to a larger room.

arch - a curved structure that spans an open space. Arches can be round or pointed and provide support to the material above them and may also support walls. But some arches are just ornamental.

architecture - the art or science of building. It includes the designing, planning, and constructing of buildings. An architect performs or oversees these activities. Architecture may also refer to a specific style or construction method.

ashlar - a hewn or squared stone.

astronomical - of or relating to astronomy.

atrium - a multi-storied court in a building that usually has a skylight.

auditorium - a room, hall, or building used for public gatherings.

basilica - an Early Christian church. It was based on a Roman building that was rectangular, had rows of columns on either side, and had a broad central aisle that ended in a semicircular area.

battlement - a long wall built on top of a castle's tower. It had a series of openings through which soldiers could shoot the enemy.

belfry - a bell tower. It is usually attached to another structure, such as a church.

bough - a large tree branch.

calligraphy - artistic or elegant handwriting.

campanile - a freestanding bell tower.

cast iron - a hard, brittle kind of iron that is formed in a mold.

cathedral - any large or important church.

citadel - a fortress that overlooks a city.

communal - something shared by many members of a community.

Corinthian column - the most elaborately decorated of the three Greek columns. It has acanthus leaves carved on the top.

corridor - a long hallway in a building. It usually has rooms opening onto it.

courtyard - an open area surrounded by walls. Courtyards are usually in or next to a large building.

cross beam - any large beam that crosses another or that crosses from wall to wall.

Crusades - military expeditions undertaken by European Christians in the eleventh, twelfth, and thirteenth centuries. They wanted to win the Holy Land from the Muslims.

Cyclopean masonry - a style of stone construction that uses large, irregular blocks without mortar.

cylindrical - something that resembles a cylinder in shape.

Dalai Lama - the spiritual and political leader of the Buddhists of Tibet.

debut - the first public appearance.

declination - leaning, bending, or sloping downward.

dirigible - a rigid, cigar-shaped airship driven by motors and capable of being steered.

distort - to twist or bend something out of shape.

dome - a round roof resembling a hemisphere. Domes are built on a circular or many-sided base.

Doric column - the simplest of the three Greek columns. It has a plain top and no base.

duct - a pipe, tube, or channel that carries gases or liquids.

dynamic - something that is full of energy, vigor, and force.

eclectic - selecting the best elements from different sources.

efficient - to bring about a desired event using little effort or wasted resources.

establishment - the settling of an area.

exterior - the outside surface of something, such as a building.

fan vault - a Gothic vault in which the ribs from each springer spread out like the vanes of a fan.

fiberglass - glass fibers used to make products, especially insulation.

floor plan - a map of a building.

flying buttress - an arched support between the wall of a building and a pier or other structure. It helps the wall bear the weight of the roof.

fortify - to make something strong.

foundation - the base of a building.

foundry - a place where metal is melted and poured into molds.

frame - the structure that gives a building its shape.

fresco - the art or method of painting on a surface of wet plaster.

frieze - a decorative, horizontal band around the top of a wall or building.

geometric - something that is decorated with straight lines, angles, circles, triangles, or similar forms.

Georgian - an English style of architecture used in the eighteenth century. It featured Palladian and Neoclassic styles.

glass curtain wall - a glass wall attached to the exterior of a building. It does not support any of the building's weight.

glaze - a smooth, glossy coating.

granite - a hard, durable igneous rock that is often used in building construction.

hammerbeam roof - a roof made of trusses that could span great distances.

hangar - a building for storing and repairing aircraft.

indigenous - a description of something or someone who is native to a certain place.

Industrial Age - a time of changes in economies and lifestyles. It began in England in the late eighteenth century. Factories and machines were developed to manufacture goods. Oil, steam, and electric power replaced human power.

industrialization - to set up or develop industries in a place.

innovation - a new idea or method.

insulation - a material placed between the exterior and interior walls of a building. It prevents the passage of heat.

interlock - to lock or fit together closely.

Ionic columns - one of the three types of Greek columns. It has scrolls carved on the top.

Koran - the sacred book of the Muslim religion.

lamella dome - a dome made from a thin, flat material.

lattice frame - a framework of crossed metal or wood strips.

lime - a solid material consisting of calcium oxide, often with magnesium oxide, that is used in building and agriculture.

limestone - a rock formed chiefly by accumulated organic remains, such as shells, and calcium carbonate. Limestone yields lime when burned.

low-pitch roof - a roof that does not have much slope.

masonry - work done with stone, brick, and mortar.

masterpiece - work done with extraordinary skill, a supreme intellectual or artistic achievement.

medieval - something that relates to the Middle Ages, a period of European history from about A.D. 500 to 1500.

mesh - a woven knotted or knit material with evenly spaced holes.

minaret - a slender, high tower on a Muslim mosque that has balconies on it. From the balconies, people are called to prayer.

moat - a trench around a building or a castle that is usually filled with water.

molten - liquefied by heat.

mortar - a building material made by mixing cement, lime, or gypsum with sand and water that hardens and is used in masonry or plastering.

mosaic - a picture made up of many small pieces of material such as glass or stone.

nave - the long, narrow, central hall of a cross-shaped church.

octagonal - a closed figure with eight angles and eight sides.

onion dome - a dome that has the general shape of an onion.

pagoda - a tower many stories high in the Far East that is built as a memorial or temple. Pagodas have a roof between each story that curves upward.

Palladian - in the style of architect Andrea Palladio.

panoramic - a view of an area that is unobstructed in all directions.

pier - a vertical support that holds up the end of an arch.

pilaster - a rectangular, flat column that projects slightly from the wall.

planetarium - a place with an ocular device that projects celestial images and effects.

plate glass - a big sheet of glass that has been rolled, ground, and polished.

podium - a raised platform from which to address an audience.

polyester - a light, man-made resin that is used to make fiber. This fiber is then woven into fabric.

pozzolana - a siliceous material that reacts with lime and water to form a slow-hardening cement.

prefabricated - something that is made up in advance. Also, standardized parts made for easy and rapid assembly.

reinforced concrete - concrete that has metal embedded into it.

relief sculpture - sculpture that is carved onto a surface so that it projects out from it.

Renaissance - a revival of art and learning that began in Italy during the fourteenth century, marked by a renewed interest in Greek and Latin literature and art.

ribbed dome - a dome that is built in sections between ribs.

rivet - a bolt that has a head on one end and is flat on the other end. It is passed through two pieces of metal and then pressed on the flat end to form a second head.

Romanesque - The style of architecture widely used in western Europe in the eleventh and twelfth centuries, characterized by massive stone construction, rounded arches and vaults, and elaborate ornamentation.

rotunda - a large round building, usually with a domed roof.

safety elevator - an elevator with an automatic brake.

sandstone - rock that is usually quartz held together with silica or calcium carbonate.

sanitation - promotion of health, hygiene, and disease prevention by promoting cleanliness.

scaffolding - a temporary platform next to a building that workers sit or stand on when working above ground level.

scholar - a person who attends school or studies under a teacher.

semiprecious - a stone, such as a garnet, that is worth less than a precious stone, such as a diamond.

setback - step-like recessions in the facade of a building near the top.

skylight - an opening in the roof of a building that is covered with a transparent material that lets in light.

soapstone - a soft stone with a soapy feel that is made of mostly talc, chlorite, and magnetite.

sophisticated - developed to a highly complex level.

spacious - a place that is roomy and not crowded.

span - a large amount of space between supports.

stave - a long, narrow strip of wood.

stud - an upright piece in the frame of a building to which sheetrock, paneling, or laths are attached.

subterranean - beneath the surface of the earth.

symmetry - being equal on both sides of a center line. Something is asymmetrical if the two sides are unequal.

technique - a method or manner of bringing about a desired result in science, art, sports, or profession.

Teflon - a man-made fluorine-containing resin used for coating articles to prevent sticking.

terrace - a group of houses or apartments built on raised or sloping ground.

tier - two or more rows arranged one above the other.

translucent - material that lets light through but is not clear.

truss - a framework of wood used to support a heavy load, such as a roof.

vaulting - constructed with vaults.

ventilation - a system or means of providing fresh air.

wattle and daub - a framework of woven rods and twigs plastered with clay.

whitewashed - painted with whitewash, a mixture of lime and water.

wrought iron - a commercial form of iron that is tough but easily worked.

INTERNET SITES

The Great Buildings Collection
http://www.greatbuildings.com/
The Great Buildings Collection is a gateway to architecture from around the world and across history. The Great Buildings Collection documents hundreds of buildings and leading architects with 3D models, photographic images, and architectural drawings, plus commentaries, bibliographies, and web links, for famous designers and structures of all kinds.

The Chicago Athenaeum: Museum of Architecture and Design
http://www.chi-athenaeum.org/
As the nation's only independent museum of architecture and design, the Chicago Athenaeum has demonstrated leadership and innovation in bringing the subject of design and its impact on the quality of life before a worldwide audience.

Architecture Online
http://architecture.simplenet.com/
Architecture Online is a site dedicated to Architecture in both the practical and academic realms. Included on this site are major works from modern architects in Europe and America, links to architects on the Web, links to schools of architecture, and a tour of the Villa Savoye.

These sites are subject to change. Go to your favorite search engine and try "architecture" for more sites.

FOR FURTHER READING

Adam, Robert. *Buildings: How They Work*. New York: Sterling Publications, 1995.

Gardner, Robert. *Architecture: Yesterday's Science, Today's Technology*. New York: Twenty-First Century Books, 1995.

MacDonald, Fiona. *A Medieval Cathedral*. New York: Peter Bedrick Books, 1991.

Wilkinson, Philip. *Amazing Buildings*. New York: Dorling Kindersley, 1993.

INDEX